Creative PIANO SOLO

CHRISTMAS CAROLS

Unique, Distinctive Piano Arrangements of 20 Holiday Favorites

ISBN 978-1-4950-2656-0

HAL•LEONARD® CORPORATION

7777 W. BLUEMOUND RD. P.O. BOX 13819 MILWAUKEE, WI 53213

In Australia Contact:
Hal Leonard Australia Pty. Ltd.
4 Lentara Court
Cheltenham, Victoria, 3192 Australia
Email: ausadmin@halleonard.com.au

Visit Hal Leonard Online at
www.halleonard.com

CONTENTS

ANGELS WE HAVE HEARD ON HIGH

Traditional French Carol
Translated by JAMES CHADWICK

To Coda ⊕

AULD LANG SYNE

Words by ROBERT BURNS
Traditional Scottish Melody

Slowly, very freely

Slowly, very freely (♩♩ = ♩♩)

molto rit.   ***mp***

8va‑‑‑‑‑‑‑‑‑‑‑‑‑

AWAY IN A MANGER

Anonymous Text (v.1,2)
Text by JOHN T. McFARLAND (v.3)
Music by JONATHAN E. SPILLMAN

Moderately fast

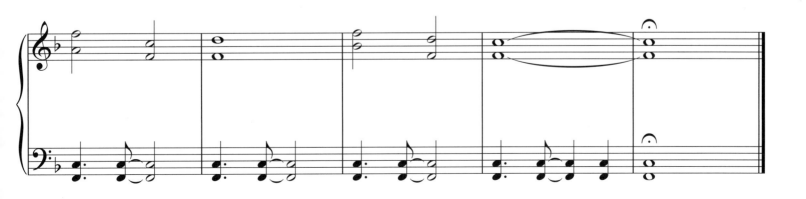

COVENTRY CAROL

Words by ROBERT CROO
Traditional English Melody

Moderately, expressively

p

DECK THE HALL

Traditional Welsh Carol

THE FIRST NOËL

17th Century English Carol
Music from W. Sandys' *Christmas Carols*

Tempo I

GOD REST YE MERRY, GENTLEMEN

19th Century English Carol

In 2, freely moving

In 2, steady ($\quad = \quad .$)

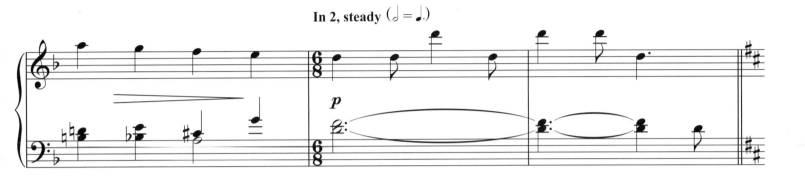

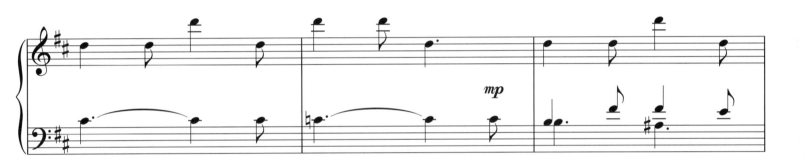

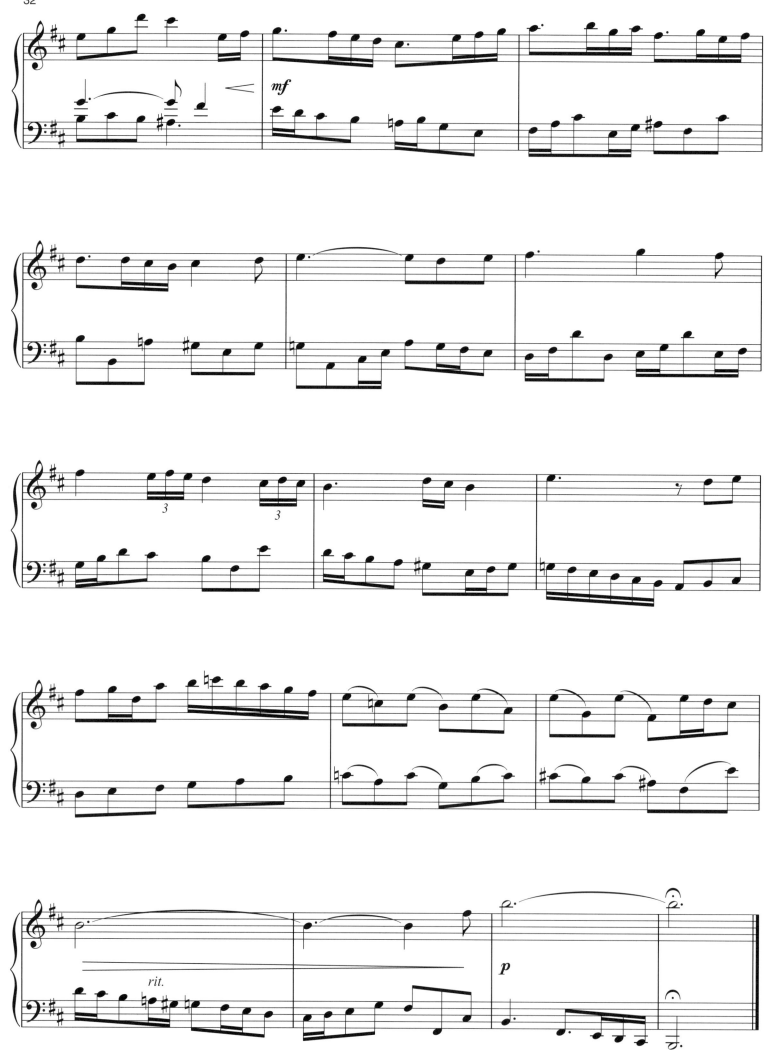

HARK! THE HERALD ANGELS SING

Words by CHARLES WESLEY
Altered by GEORGE WHITEFIELD
Music by FELIX MENDELSSOHN-BARTHOLDY
Arranged by WILLIAM H. CUMMINGS

HERE WE COME A-WASSAILING

Traditional

IT CAME UPON THE MIDNIGHT CLEAR

Words by EDMUND HAMILTON SEARS
Music by RICHARD STORRS WILLIS

8vb

JINGLE BELLS

Words and Music by
J. PIERPONT

To Coda ⊕

JOY TO THE WORLD

Words by ISAAC WATTS
Music by GEORGE FRIDERIC HANDEL
Adapted by LOWELL MASON

O COME, ALL YE FAITHFUL
(Adeste Fideles)

Music by JOHN FRANCIS WADE
Latin Words translated by FREDERICK OAKELEY

Gently flowing, in two

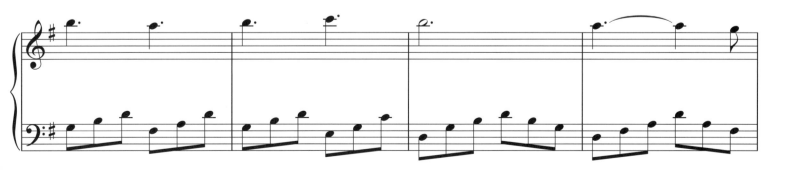

O CHRISTMAS TREE

Traditional German Carol

In a Baroque Style

O HOLY NIGHT

French Words by PLACIDE CAPPEAU
English Words by JOHN S. DWIGHT
Music by ADOLPHE ADAM

Moderately, flowing in 2

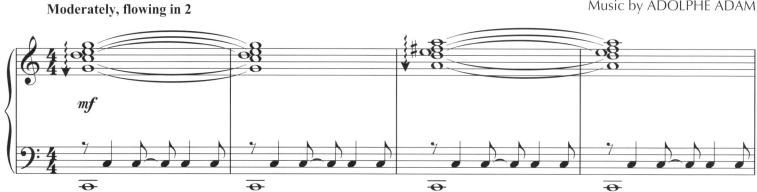

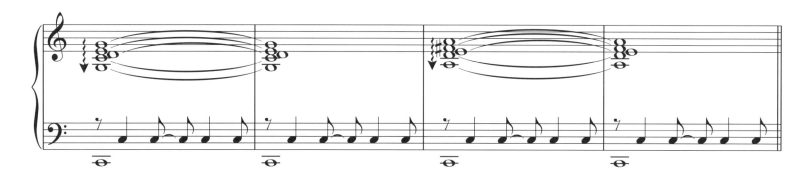

O LITTLE TOWN OF BETHLEHEM

Words by PHILLIPS BROOKS
Music by LEWIS H. REDNER

Moderato sostenuto

SILENT NIGHT

Words by JOSEPH MOHR
Translated by JOHN F. YOUNG
Music by FRANZ X. GRUBER

UP ON THE HOUSETOP

Words and Music by
B.R. HANBY

Moderately fast Bluegrass

WE THREE KINGS OF ORIENT ARE

Words and Music by
JOHN H. HOPKINS, Jr.

Moderato, mysterioso

WHAT CHILD IS THIS?

Words by WILLIAM C. DIX
16th Century English Melody

Joyfully